THE CREATIVE SOLOIST

Fourteen original and unique vocal solos for medium voice
by Marjorie Jones

Gentry Publications

Distributed by Alexandria House, Box 300, Alexandria, IN 46001-0300

The Teacher

LESLIE HILL*

MARJORIE JONES

*Used by permission

faint the flick - er, and how low the can - dles of my know-ledge glow.

I teach them pow'r to will and do, but

on - ly now to learn a - new my own great weak-ness through and through.

I

What Can I Give Him?

CHRISTINA ROSSETTI

MARJORIE JONES

6

8

The Blades of Grass

STEPHEN CRANE

MARJORIE JONES

10

11

A Knight of Bethlehem

H.N. MAUGHAM*

MARJORIE JONES

*from "*Masterpieces of Religious Verse*," Harper & Row, publishers. Used by permission

Digging

ROBERT G. BENSON*

MARJORIE JONES

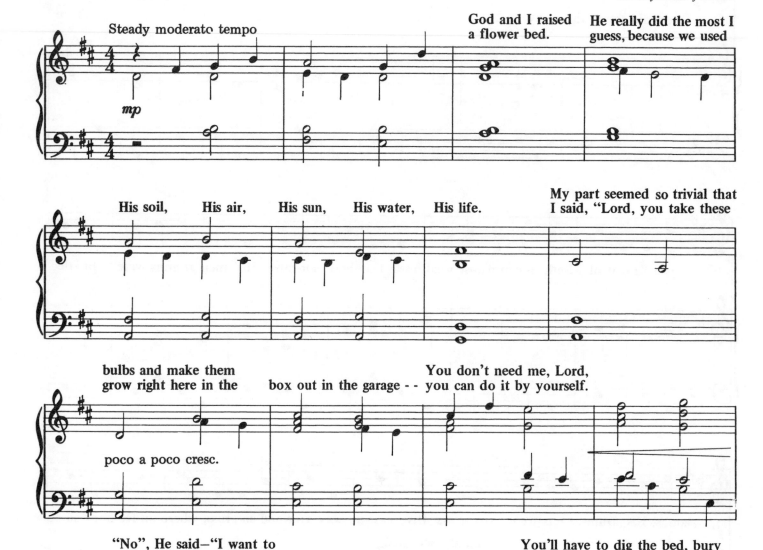

Steady moderate tempo

God and I raised a flower bed. He really did the most I guess, because we used

His soil, His air, His sun, His water, His life. My part seemed so trivial that I said, "Lord, you take these

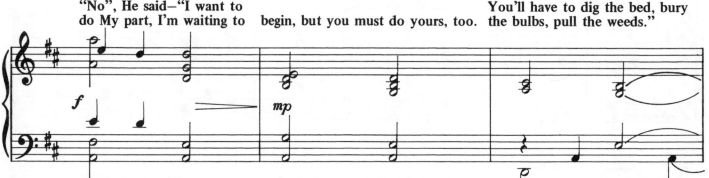

bulbs and make them grow right here in the box out in the garage - - You don't need me, Lord, you can do it by yourself.

"No", He said—"I want to do My part, I'm waiting to begin, but you must do yours, too. You'll have to dig the bed, bury the bulbs, pull the weeds."

"Well, all right," I said, and I did my feeble part, and God took those bulbs, burst them with life, fed them with soil, showered them with rain,

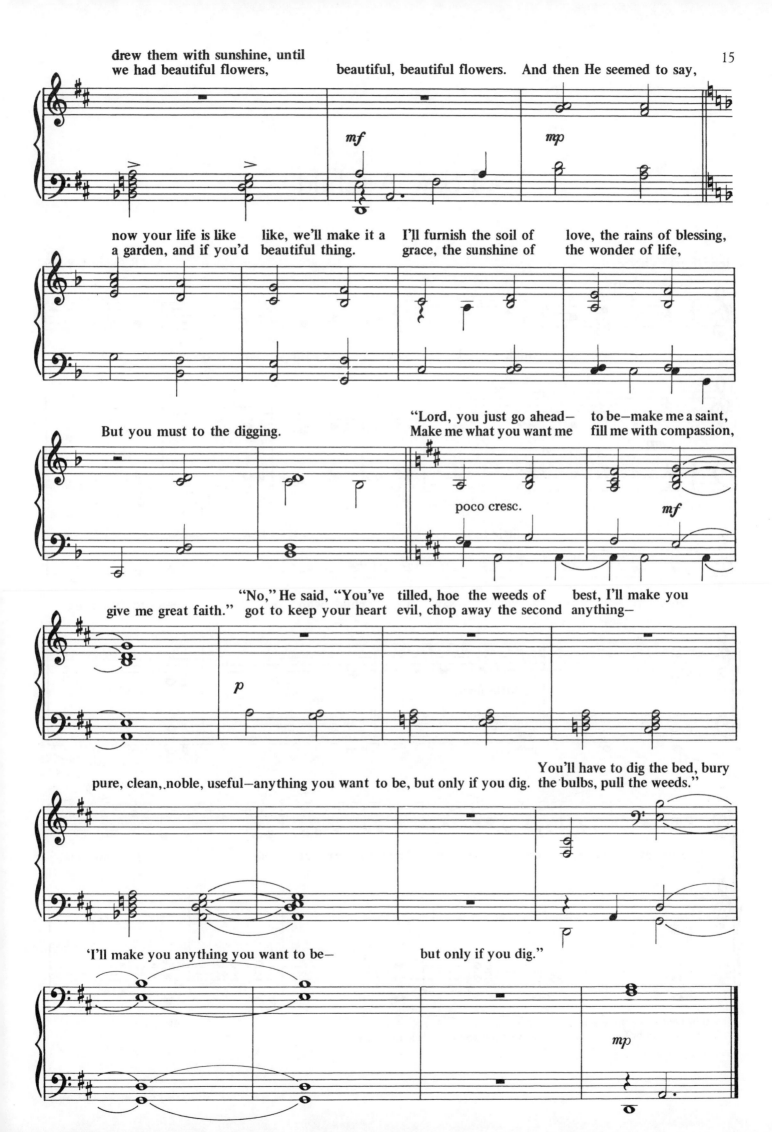

I Saw A Child

JESSIE STEVENS*

MARJORIE JONES

poco accel.   poco a poco cresc.

I saw a man whose heart rose in Him like a great ground

swell_____ be-cause He heard the mad laugh of a boy_____

_____ who had ne-ver cried!_____ I saw this

man; He was nailed half-way be-tween hea-ven and earth,

Half-way be-tween hea-ven and earth the God-man hung, buy-ing back His child,_____

_____ I saw the child,_____ I saw the man, and

God has seen to it that I shall not find rest_____ un - til boy and man are

in each o - thers' arms, laugh - ing and cry - ing.

Ten Little Christians

UNKNOWN

MARJORIE JONES

22

eight.   Eight splen-did Chris-tians, but   no-thing rhymes with six - teen.   So we

sim - ply note that in sev-en more verses there would be one thousand and twenty-four Chris-tians. One

thousand and twenty - four ___ Chris - tians, which would be quite a church full.

And it   all   be - gan with   one.

Others

M.J.

MARJORIE JONES

I have been un-lov-ing, _____ and in my want-ing to be un-der-

stood I have not un-der-stood, the need for un-der-stand-ing you.

In my struggling for ac-cept-ance I have not ac-cept-ed oth-ers as they

are. In my long-ing to be loved I have been un-lov-ing, _____

_____ and in my want-ing to be un-der-stood I have not un-der-stood the

need for un-der-stand-ing you. _____ I pray that God might

keep me so a-ware of those a-round me that I for-get my-self and seek

poco a poco cresc. *f* *poco a poco dim.*

on-ly to share His love, ___ and that in my de-spond-en-cy I might

p *mp* *p* *mp*

draw up-on His joy, and give His love and joy to you. _____ I

pray that He might keep me so a-ware of those a-round me.

p *rit.* *p* *pp*

Four Short Solos

ADELAIDE CRAPSEY*   MARJORIE JONES

I. On Seeing Weather-beaten Trees

On see - ing weath-er-beat - en trees. _____ Is

it as plain - ly by our liv - ing shown;

By slant and twist which way the wind hath

blown. _____ On see - ing weath-er-beat - en trees.

II. November Night

Lis - ten... with faint dry sound, Like steps of pass-ing ghosts, _

_ The leaves, _ frost crisped, break from the trees and fall.

III. Triad

These be three si - lent things: The fall - ing snow,

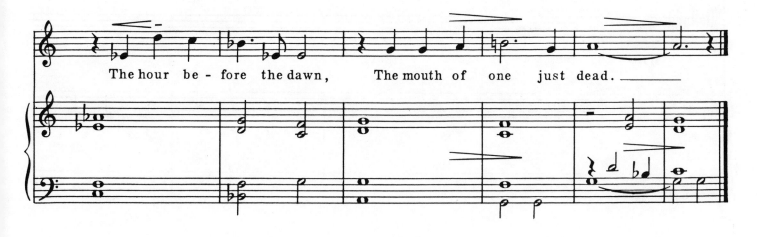

The hour be - fore the dawn, The mouth of one just dead. _

30

IV. Little Sister Rose-Marie

Lit - tle sis - ter Rose - Ma - rie, Will thy voice as bird - note clear

Bring out melody

Lift and rip - ple o - ver Heav - en; As its mor - tal

sound is giv - en, Swift bird voice, so young and clear? How God will be

glad of thee, Lit - tle sis - ter Rose - Ma - rie.

It Couldn't Be Done

JACKIE KANNON

MARJORIE JONES

Rain

PHILIP LAZARUS*

MARJORIE JONES

Is -n't it jol - ly to walk in the rain?___

Is-n't it a jol - ly thing to walk in the rain, To chuc-kle and chor-tle and talk in the rain. Is - n't it jol - ly to

Accented

walk in the rain, To chuck - le and chor - tle and

talk in the rain, Splat - tered and splashed from our

head to **our** toe._____ Is - n't it jol - ly?

Slower

No!